Journaling Your
Personal Walk
with
God

A Devotional Journal

Draw nigh to God and he
will draw nigh to you.
(James 4:8a)

Sara A. Davis

Printed in the United States of America

ISBN: 978-0-9827151-9-2

Published by Lowbar Publishing Company
Nashville, Tennessee 37204
615-972-2842
E-mail: Lowbar@comcast.net
Website: www.lowbarbookstore.com

Layout Designer: Norah S. Branch
Graphic art and book Cover Designer: Norah S. Branch

Excerpts from the King James and New International Version of the Bible

Journaling Your Personal Walk with God

A personal repository to treasure as you walk close with God

START DATE:

_____

END DATE:

_____

"Study to show thyself approved unto God,
a workman that needeth not to be ashamed,
rightly dividing the word of truth."
2 Timothy 2:15

Personal Information

Name: _____

Address: _____

_____

City: _____

State: _____

Zip: _____

Telephone: (H)_____

(C) _____

E-mail:_____

••

Pastor: _____

Church: _____

Address: _____

_____

City:_____

State: _____

Zip: _____

Telephone: (H) _____

(C) _____

Website:_____

Prayer Partners

Name: _____

Telephone: (H) _____

(C) _____

E-mail:_____

Name: _____

Telephone: (H) _____

(C) _____

E-mail:_____

Name: _____

Telephone: (H) _____

(C) _____

E-mail:_____

Name: _____

Telephone: (H) _____

(C) _____

E-mail:_____

Name: _____

Telephone: (H) _____

(C) _____

E-mail:_____

"Praying always with all prayer and supplication in the Spirit,
and watching thereunto with all perseverance and supplication for all saints:"
(Ephesians 6:18)

Daily Confession

Who I am in Jesus Christ

I am God's workmanship.
For we are God's handiwork, created in Christ Jesus to do good works, which God prepared in advance for us to do.
(Ephesians 2:10)

I am a new creature in Christ.
Therefore, if anyone is in Christ, the new creation has come: The old has gone, the new is here!
(2 Corinthians 5:17)

I am a joint-heir with Christ.
Now if we are children, then we are heirs—heirs of God and co-heirs with Christ, if indeed we share in his sufferings in order that we may also share in his glory.
(Romans 8:17)

I am an ambassador for Christ.
We are therefore Christ's ambassadors, as though God were making his appeal through us. We implore you on Christ's behalf: Be reconciled to God.
(2 Corinthians 5:20)

I am a chosen generation, a royal priesthood, a holy nation.
But you are a chosen people, a royal priesthood, a holy nation, God's special possession, that you may declare the praises of him who called you out of darkness into his wonderful light.
(1 Peter 2:9)

Daily Confession

I am the righteousness of God in Jesus Christ.
God made him who had no sin to be sin for us, so that in him
we might become the righteousness of God.

(2 Corinthians 5:21)

I am the temple of the Holy Spirit; I am not my own.
Do you not know that your body is the temple of the Holy
Spirit, which is in you, which you have received from God?

(1 Corinthians 6:19)

I am a child of God.
Yet to all who did receive him, to those who believed in his
name, he gave the right to become children of God.

(John 1:12)

I am more than a conqueror in Christ.
Who shall separate us from the love of Christ? Shall trouble
or hardship or persecution or famine or nakedness or danger
or sword? As it is written: "For your sake we face death all
day long; we are considered as sheep to be slaughtered."
No, in all these things we are more than conquerors through
him who loved us.

(Romans 8:35-37)

I can do all things through Christ.
I have learned the secret of being content in any and every situation, whether well fed or hungry, whether living in
plenty or in want. I can do all this through Him who gives
me strength.

(Philippians 4:12-13)

Table of Contents

How to Benefit from Journaling

This devotional journal is designed to enhance your study of the Word of God. It will help cultivate a good habit to assist in your spiritual development. God is doing awesome things in the lives of His people. Cherish the moments, record the moments, and share them with the next generation by utilizing this unique book.

Using this journal will help you to:

- Recall the promises of God so your faith will not waver

- Know the benefits of a closer walk with God

- Grow spiritually and stand in the midst of adversity

- Cherish the Word of God by recording notes during worship services, Bible study classes and seminars

- Enhance your understanding of praying to a heavenly Father

- Record moments of witnessing experiences

"Thy word is a lamp unto my feet,
and a light unto my path."
(Psalm 119:105)

Love

"For God so loved the world that he gave
his only begotten Son, that whosoever
believeth in him should not perish,
but have everlasting life."
John 3:16

Introduction

Writing is a form of communication and a way of recording information. God demonstrated the importance of writing to Moses: "And Moses turned, and went down from the mount, and the two tables of the testimony were in his hand: the tables were written on both their sides; on the one side and on the other were they written. And the tables were the work of God and the writing was the writing of God, graven upon the tables." (Exodus 32:15-16). As ancient nations and communities were being developed, people realized the benefits of writing. Today, technological advances have further expanded the modalities of documenting. By using this book you can further propel into spiritual maturity as you learn, read, pray, study, and record the Word of God.

The Bible is a book of divine instructions, providing daily inspirations for our every need. The Word of God tells us that:

> "All scripture is given by inspiration of God, and is profitable for doctrine, for reproof, for correction, for instruction in righteousness; That the man of God may be perfect, thoroughly furnished unto all good works." (2 Timothy 3:16-17)

> "For the word of God is quick, and powerful, sharper than any two edged sword, piercing even to the dividing asunder of soul and spirit, and of the joints and marrow, and is a discerner of the thoughts and intents of the heart." (Hebrews 4:12)

If you do not usually take notes during Bible study, start today by using this unique and handy book as a guide. May God continue to bless you through the study of His Word, and remember to keep God first in your life.

Promises

"For all the promises of God in him
are yea, and in him Amen,
unto the glory of God by us."
2 Corinthians 1:20

Words of Promise

"For all the promises of God in him are yea, and in him Amen, unto the glory of God by us."

(2 Corinthians1:20)

The Word of God comes and works in the hearts of those who believe when they hear or read it. Therefore, cherish the Word of God and apply it to your daily living, as stated in 2 Peter 1:4 : "Whereby are given unto us exceeding great and precious promises: that by these ye might be par-takers of the divine nature, having escaped the corruption that is in the world through lust." When faced with trials, distress, or perplexity of the spirit, let us be reminded of what the Word of God says. Learn to meditate upon and apply His word in every situation.

Deuteronomy 31:6 Be strong and of a good courage, fear not, nor be afraid of them: for the LORD thy God, he it is that doth go with thee; he will not fail thee, nor forsake thee.

Psalm 34:10 The young lions do lack, and suffer hunger, but they that seek the Lord shall not want any good thing.

Psalm 34:15 The eyes of the LORD are upon the righteous, and his ears are open unto their cry.

Psalm 37:3-4 Trust in the Lord, and do good; so shalt thou dwell in the land, and verily thou shalt be fed. Delight thyself also in the Lord; and he shall give thee the desires of thine heart.

Psalm 37:39 But the salvation of the righteous is of the Lord; he is their strength in the time of trouble.

Psalm 40:1 I waited patiently for the Lord; and he inclined unto me, and heard my cry.

Psalm 46:1 God is our refuge and strength, a very present help in trouble.

Psalm 46:10	Be still, and know that I am God; I will be exalted among the heathen, I will be exalted in the earth.
Psalm 55:22	Cast thy burden upon the LORD, and he shall sustain thee: he shall never suffer the righteous to be moved.
Proverbs 16:7	When a man's ways please the LORD, he maketh even his enemies to be at peace with him.
Isaiah 26:3	Thou wilt keep him in perfect peace, whose mind is stayed on thee; because he trusteth in thee.
John 10:9	I am the door: by me if any man enter in, he shall be saved, and shall go in and out, and find pasture.
Luke 10:19	Behold, I give unto you power to tread on serpents and scorpions, and over all the power of the enemy: and nothing shall by any means hurt you.
Luke 18:27	And he said, The things which are impossible with men are possible with God.
John 14:27	Peace I leave with you, my peace I give unto you: not as the world giveth, give I unto you. Let not your heart be troubled, neither let it be afraid.
John 15:7	If ye abide in me, and my words abide in you, ye shall ask what ye will, and it shall be done unto you.
Romans 8:28	And we know that all things work together for good to them that love God, to them who are the called according to his purpose.
Romans 8:31	What shall we then say to these things, If God be for us, who can be against us?
Romans 8:37	Nay, in all these things we are more than conquerors through him that loved us.
Romans 12:2	And be not conformed to this world: but be ye transformed by the renewing of your mind, that ye may prove what is that good, and acceptable, and perfect, will of God.

Romans 15:13	Now the God of hope fill you with all joy and peace in believing, that ye may abound in hope, through the power of the Holy Ghost.
2 Corinthians 9:8	And God is able to make all grace abound toward you; that ye, always having all sufficiency in all things, may abound to every good work:
Philippians 1:6	Being confident of this very thing, that he which hath begun a good work in you will perform it until the day of Jesus Christ.
Philippians 4:13	I can do all things through Christ which strengtheneth me.
Philippians 4:19	But my God shall supply all your need according to his riches in glory by Christ Jesus.
James 1:5	If any of you lack wisdom, let him ask of God, that giveth to all men liberally, and upbraideth not, and it shall be given him.
Hebrews 10:23	Let us hold fast the profession of our faith without wavering (for he is faithful that promised).
Hebrews 13:5	Let your conversation be without covetousness; and be content with such things as ye have: for he hath said, I will never leave thee, nor forsake thee.
Hebrews 13:6	So that we may boldly say, The Lord is my helper, and I will not fear what man shall do unto me.

My Promises

My Promises

My Promises

My Promises

Fellowship

"But if we walk in the light, as he is in the light,
we have fellowship one with another,
and the blood of Jesus Christ
his Son cleanseth us from all sin."
1 John 1:7

Walking Closer with God

"But if we walk in the light, as he is in the light, we have fellowship one with another, and the blood of Jesus Christ his Son cleanseth us from all sin." (1 John 1:7)

❖ Building a Relationship

Walking closely with someone requires building a relationship with them. In order to build a relationship with someone, you have to spend quality time together. When you invest your time, effort, and trust in building a relationship, you expect something in return. What do you do when your expectations are not met? Do you lose faith in the relationship?

- What were the motives of the relationship?
- How many promises were made but never fulfilled?
- How many of those promises ended with hurtful pains?
- How many open wounds still need to be healed?

The Word of God says in Proverbs 14:12: "There is a way which seemeth right unto a man, but the end thereof are the ways of death." Therefore, when we walk obediently and intimately with God, He will fulfill all His promises.

❖ Take a Closer Walk with God and Realize the Benefits

The spirit man yearns for the intimacy and presence of God. This yearning is filled as we spend quality time in the Word of God, scripture mediation, prayer, and thanksgiving. The scripture tells us in Jeremiah 1:5 that, "Before I formed thee in the belly I knew thee; and before thou camest forth out of the womb I sanctified thee, and I ordained thee a prophet unto the nations."

Let's keep in mind that man was created for God's glory. "Even every one that is called by my name: for I have created him for my glory, I have formed him; yea, I have made him." Isaiah 43:7. We were created to be used by God; therefore, we must let our lives connect with His Word. An intimate relationship with God requires spending time in the Bible. John 1:1 tells us that, "In the beginning was the Word and the Word was with God, and the Word was God." Walking closely to God means walking in His Word. Psalm 73:28 says, "But it is good for me to draw near to God: ..." and Hebrews 10:22 gives this instruction to believers: "Let us draw near with a true heart in full assurance of faith, having our hearts sprinkled from an evil conscience, and our bodies washed with pure water."

On a daily basis, it is essential to:
- Study the Word
- Receive the Word
- Pray the Word
- Trust the Word
- Offer Thanks
- Walk in the Word

The preceding and following scriptures are listed as reminders of the benefits in walking more closely with God. It is my prayer and desire that you will be encouraged to do further reading and searching in the Word, as you realize why a closer walk with God is important to you and your family.

❖ Benefits of Studying

"All scripture is given by inspiration of God, and is profitable for doctrine, for reproof, for correction, for instruction in righteousness; That the man of God may be perfect, thoroughly furnished unto all good works." **(2 Timothy 3:16-17)**

"Study to show thyself approved unto God, a workman that needeth not to be ashamed, rightly dividing the word of truth." **(2 Timothy 2:15)**
"For the word of God is quick, and powerful, and sharper than any two edged sword, piercing even to the dividing asunder of soul and spirit, and of the joints and marrow, and is a discerner of the thoughts and intents of the heart." **(Hebrews 4:12)**

"Thy word is a lamp unto my feet, and a light unto my path." **(Psalm 119:10)**

❖ Benefits of Receiving

"Wherefore lay apart all filthiness and superfluity of naughtiness, and receive with meekness the engrafted word, which is able to save your souls." **(James 1:21)**

"But these are written, that ye might believe that Jesus is the Christ, the Son of God; and that believing ye might have life through his name." **(John 20:31)**

"And I will pray the Father, and he shall give you another Comforter, that he may abide with you forever." **(John 14:16)**

❖ Benefits of Praying

"And he spake a parable unto them to this end, that men ought always to pray, and not to faint." **(Luke 18:1)**

"And whatsoever ye shall ask in my name, that will I do, that the Father may be glorified in the Son." **(John 14:13)**

"Confess your faults one to another, and pray one for another, that ye may be healed. The effectual fervent prayer of a righteous man availeth much." **(James 5:15)**

"And this is the confidence that we have in him, that, if we ask any thing according to his will, he heareth us:" **(1 John 5:14)**

"Be careful for nothing; but in every thing by prayer and supplication with thanksgiving let your requests be made known unto God." **(Philippians 4:6)**

❖ Benefits of Trusting

"For the scripture saith, Whosoever believeth on him shall not be ashamed." **(Romans 10:11)**

"Blessed is the man that trusteth in the LORD, and whose hope the LORD is. For he shall be as a tree planted by the waters, and that spreadeth out her roots by the river, and shall not see when heat cometh, but her leaf shall be green; and shall not be careful in the year of drought, neither shall cease from yielding fruit." **(Jeremiah 17:7-8)**

"Trust in the LORD with all thine heart; and lean not unto thine own understanding. In all thy ways acknowledge him, and he shall direct thy paths." **(Proverbs 3:5-6)**

❖ Benefits of Offering Thanks

"It is a good thing to give thanks unto the Lord, and to sing praises unto thy name, O most high." **(Psalm 92:1)**

"O give thanks unto the LORD; for he is good; for his mercy endureth for ever." **(1 Chronicles 16:34)**

"Giving thanks unto the Father, which hath made us meet to be partakers of the inheritance of the saints in light." **(Colossians 1:12)**

"In every thing give thanks: for this is the will of God in Christ Jesus concerning you." **(1 Thessalonians 5:18)**

❖ Benefits of Walking with the Lord

"For the LORD God is a sun and shield: the LORD will give grace and glory: no good thing will he withhold from them that walk uprightly." **(Psalm 84:11)**

"Blessed is every one that feareth the LORD; that walketh in his ways." **(Psalm 128:1)**

"See then that ye walk circumspectly, not as fools, but as wise, Redeeming the time, because the days are evil." **(Ephesians 5:15-16)**

"For this ye know, that no whoremonger, nor unclean person, nor covetous man, who is an idolater, hath any inheritance in the kingdom of Christ and of God. Let no man deceive you with vain words: for because of these things cometh the wrath of God upon the children of disobedience. Be not ye therefore partakers with them. For ye were sometimes darkness, but now are ye light in the Lord: walk as children of light:" **(Ephesians 5:5-8)**

Add to your FAITH

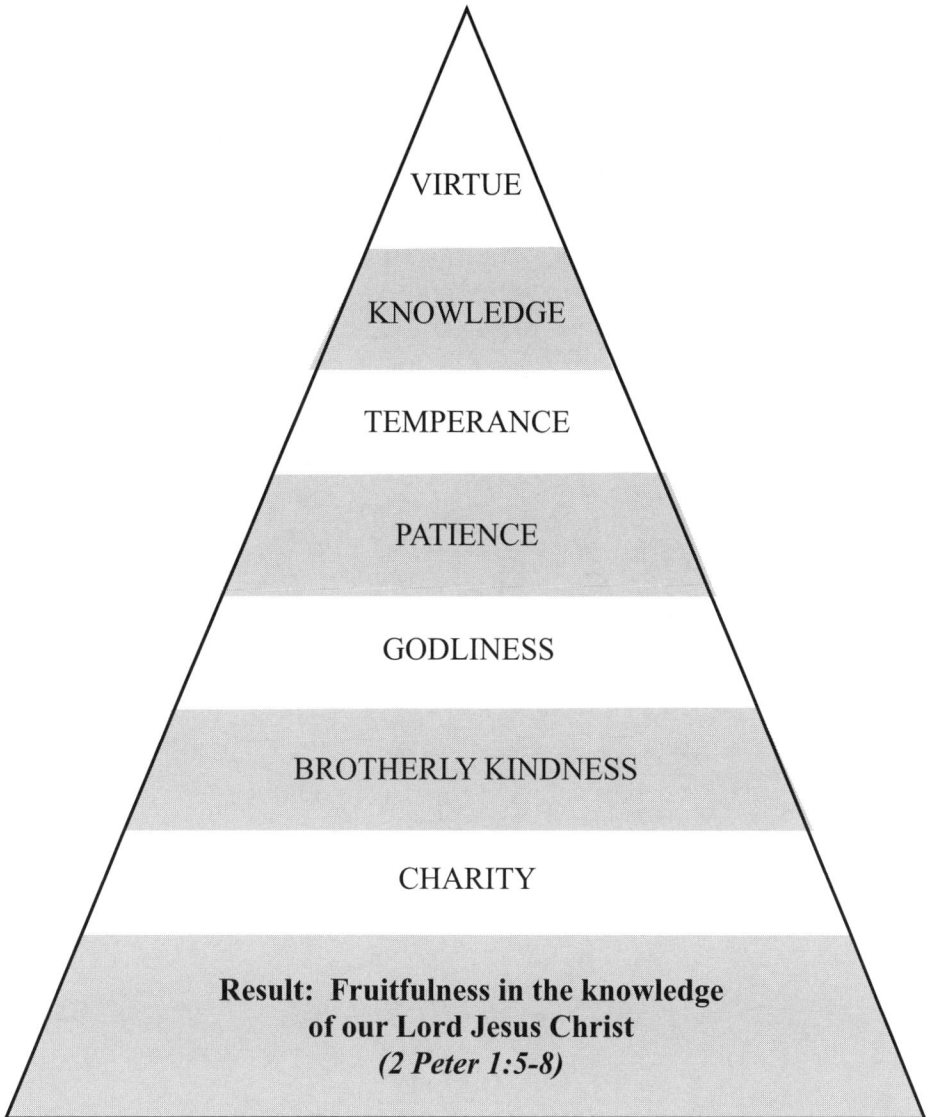

VIRTUE

KNOWLEDGE

TEMPERANCE

PATIENCE

GODLINESS

BROTHERLY KINDNESS

CHARITY

Result: Fruitfulness in the knowledge of our Lord Jesus Christ
(2 Peter 1:5-8)

Growth

"And he shall be like a tree planted
by the rivers of water, that bringeth forth
his fruit in his season; his leaf also
shall not wither; and whatsoever
he doeth shall prosper."
Psalm 1:3

Spiritual Growth

"For I know the thoughts that I think toward you, saith the LORD, thoughts of peace, and not of evil, to give you an expected end." (Jeremiah 29:11)

It is important to grow spiritually in the word of God. As we grow, our spiritual senses will become much more alert to the things of God, and cause us to lay aside the things of the flesh. We must be mindful of the qualities and virtues that should be maintained in our daily walk through life. Therefore, it is imperative to know and stand on the Word of God by memorizing and mediating on the following scriptures.

❖ Growth

"Wherefore laying aside all malice, and all guile, and hypocrisies, and envies, and all evil speakings, As newborn babes, desire the sincere milk of the word, that ye may grow thereby: If so be ye have tasted that the Lord is gracious." **(1 Peter 2:1-3)**

"That we henceforth be no more children, tossed to and fro, and carried about with every wind of doctrine, by the sleight of men, and cunning craftiness, whereby they lie in wait to deceive; But speaking the truth in love, may grow up into him in all things, which is the head, even Christ." **(Ephesians 4:14-15)**

"That ye put off concerning the former conversation the old man, which is corrupt according to the deceitful lusts; And be renewed in the spirit of your mind; And that ye put on the new man, which after God is created in righteousness and true holiness." **(Ephesians 4:22-24)**

"Be sober, be vigilant; because your adversary the devil, as a roaring lion, walketh about, seeking whom he may devour." **(1 Peter 5:8)**

❖ Armor of God

"Put on the whole armor of God, that ye may be able to stand against the wiles of the devil." **(Ephesians 6:11)**

"Wherefore take unto you the whole armor of God that ye may be able to withstand in the evil day, and having done all, to stand. Stand therefore, having your loins girt about with truth, and having on the breastplate of righteousness; And your feet shod with the preparation of the gospel of peace; Above all, taking the shield of faith, wherewith ye shall be able to quench all the fiery darts of the wicked. And take the helmet of salvation, and the sword of the Spirit, which is the word of God." **(Ephesians 6:13-17)**

"And beside this, giving all diligence, add to your faith virtue; and to virtue knowledge; And to knowledge temperance; and to temperance patience; and to patience godliness; And to godliness brotherly kindness; and to brotherly kindness charity. For if these things be in you, and abound, they make you that ye shall neither be barren nor unfruitful in the knowledge of our Lord Jesus Christ." **(2 Peter 1:5-8)**

❖ Spiritual Warfare

"For we wrestle not against flesh and blood, but against principalities, against powers, against the rulers of the darkness of this world, against spiritual wickedness in high places." **(Ephesians 6:12)**

"Now the Spirit speaketh expressly, that in the latter times some shall depart from the faith, giving heed to seducing spirits, and doctrines of devils." **(1Timothy 4:1)**

"For the weapons of our warfare are not carnal, but mighty through God to the pulling down of strongholds; Casting down imaginations, and every high thing that exalted itself against the knowledge of God, and bringing into captivity every thought to the obedience of Christ;" **(2 Corinthians 10:4-5)**

❖ Qualities and Virtues

"Keep thy heart with all diligence: for out of it are the issues of life." **(Proverbs 4:23)**

"Put on therefore, as the elect of God, holy and beloved, bowels of mercies, kindness, humbleness of mind, meekness, long-suffering; Forbearing one another, and forgiving one another, if any man have a quarrel against any; even as Christ forgave you, so also do ye. And above all these things put on charity, which is the bond of perfectness. And let the peace of God rule in your hearts, to the which also ye are called in one body; and be ye thankful." **(Colossians 3:12-15)**

"Stand fast therefore in the liberty wherewith Christ hath made us free, and be not entangled again with the yoke of bondage." **(Galatians 5:1)**

"Let your light so shine before men, that they may see your good works, and glorify your Father which is in heaven." **(Matthew 5:16)**

"Study to show thyself approved unto God, a workman that needeth not to be ashamed, rightly dividing the word of truth." **(2 Timothy 2:15)**

As we grow and walk in maturity, let our Christian growth bring glory to God by:

G – Guarding our heart
R – Resting in the Word of God
O – Opening our mind to receive the Word
W – Walking in the wisdom of God
T – Teaching the Word of God
H – Heeding to the Word of God

May we allow the Holy Spirit to control and empower our life as we continuously walk in the plan and purpose God has ordained for us.

Learn

"Take my yoke upon you, and learn of me;
for I am meek and lowly in heart:
and ye shall find rest unto your souls."
Matthew 11:29

Cherishing the Word by Note Taking

Record of scriptures and notes
from Bible study classes,
worship services, seminars, lectures,
and personal daily devotions

"For the word of the LORD is right;
and all his works are done in truth."
(Psalm 33:4)

Date:_____Speaker:_____

Topic: _____

_____

_____

_____

_____

_____

_____

_____

_____

_____

_____

_____

_____

_____

_____

_____

"Take my yoke upon you, and learn of me;
for I am meek and lowly in heart:
and ye shall find rest unto your souls."
(Matthew 11:29)

Notes

"And take the helmet of salvation, and the sword
of the Spirit, which is the word of God:"
(Ephesians 6:17)

Date:_____Speaker:_____

Topic: _____

_____

_____

_____

_____

_____

_____

_____

_____

_____

_____

_____

_____

_____

_____

_____

_____

_____

"Take my yoke upon you, and learn of me;
for I am meek and lowly in heart:
and ye shall find rest unto your souls."
(Matthew 11:29)

Notes

"How sweet are thy words unto my taste!
yea, sweeter than honey to my mouth!"
(Psalm 119:103)

Date:_____Speaker:_____

Topic: _____

_____

_____

_____

_____

_____

_____

_____

_____

_____

_____

_____

_____

_____

_____

_____

_____

*"Take my yoke upon you, and learn of me;
for I am meek and lowly in heart:
and ye shall find rest unto your souls."
(Matthew 11:29)*

Notes

Order my steps in thy word: and let not
any iniquity have dominion over me."
(Psalm 119:133)

Date:_____Speaker:_____

Topic: _____

_____

_____

_____

_____

_____

_____

_____

_____

_____

_____

_____

_____

_____

_____

_____

_____

"Take my yoke upon you, and learn of me;
for I am meek and lowly in heart:
and ye shall find rest unto your souls."
(Matthew 11:29)

Notes

"He sent his word, and healed them,
and delivered them from their destructions."
(Psalm 107:20)

Date:_____Speaker:_____

Topic: _____

_____

_____

_____

_____

_____

_____

_____

_____

_____

_____

_____

_____

_____

_____

_____

_____

"Take my yoke upon you, and learn of me;
for I am meek and lowly in heart:
and ye shall find rest unto your souls."
(Matthew 11:29)

Notes

"The grass withereth, the flower fadeth:
but the word of our God shall stand for ever."
(Isaiah 40:8)

Date:_____Speaker:_____

Topic: _____

_____

_____

_____

_____

_____

_____

_____

_____

_____

_____

_____

_____

_____

_____

_____

_____

"Take my yoke upon you, and learn of me;
for I am meek and lowly in heart:
and ye shall find rest unto your souls."
(Matthew 11:29)

Notes

"The entrance of thy words giveth light;
it giveth understanding unto the simple."
(Psalm 119:130)

Date:_____Speaker:_____

Topic: _____

_____

_____

_____

_____

_____

_____

_____

_____

_____

_____

_____

_____

_____

_____

_____

"Take my yoke upon you, and learn of me;
for I am meek and lowly in heart:
and ye shall find rest unto your souls."
(Matthew 11:29)

Notes

"Heaven and earth shall pass away,
but my words shall not pass away."
(Matthew 24:35)

Date:_____Speaker:_____

Topic: _____

_____

_____

_____

_____

_____

_____

_____

_____

_____

_____

_____

_____

_____

_____

_____

_____

"Take my yoke upon you, and learn of me;
for I am meek and lowly in heart:
and ye shall find rest unto your souls."
(Matthew 11:29)

Notes

"Apply thine heart unto instruction,
and thine ears to the words of knowledge."
(Proverbs 23:12)

Date:_____Speaker:_____

Topic: _____

_____

_____

_____

_____

_____

_____

_____

_____

_____

_____

_____

_____

_____

_____

_____

"Take my yoke upon you, and learn of me;
for I am meek and lowly in heart:
and ye shall find rest unto your souls."
(Matthew 11:29)

Notes

"All scripture is given by inspiration of God,
and is profitable for doctrine, for reproof,
for correction, for instruction in righteousness:"
(2 Timothy 3:16)

Date:_____Speaker:_____

Topic: _____

_____

_____

_____

_____

_____

_____

_____

_____

_____

_____

_____

_____

_____

_____

_____

_____

_____

"Take my yoke upon you, and learn of me;
for I am meek and lowly in heart:
and ye shall find rest unto your souls."
(Matthew 11:29)

Notes

"My son, keep my words,
and lay up my commandments with thee."
(Proverbs 7:1)

Date:_____Speaker:_____

Topic: _____

_____

_____

_____

_____

_____

_____

_____

_____

_____

_____

_____

_____

_____

_____

_____

_____

"Take my yoke upon you, and learn of me;
for I am meek and lowly in heart:
and ye shall find rest unto your souls."
(Matthew 11:29)

Notes

"Therefore shall ye lay up these my words in your heart
and in your soul, and bind them for a sign upon your hand,
that they may be as frontlets between your eyes."
(Deuteronomy 11:18)

Date:_____Speaker:_____

Topic: _____

_____

_____

_____

_____

_____

_____

_____

_____

_____

_____

_____

_____

_____

_____

_____

_____

"Take my yoke upon you, and learn of me;
for I am meek and lowly in heart:
and ye shall find rest unto your souls."
(Matthew 11:29)

"Thy word is very pure: therefore thy servant loveth it."
(Psalm 119:140)

Date:_____Speaker:_____

Topic: _____

_____

_____

_____

_____

_____

_____

_____

_____

_____

_____

_____

_____

_____

_____

_____

"Take my yoke upon you, and learn of me;
for I am meek and lowly in heart:
and ye shall find rest unto your souls."
(Matthew 11:29)

Notes

"Thy word have I hid in mine heart, that I might not sin against thee."
(Psalm 119:11)

Date:_____Speaker:_____

Topic: _____

_____

_____

_____

_____

_____

_____

_____

_____

_____

_____

_____

_____

_____

_____

_____

_____

"Take my yoke upon you, and learn of me;
for I am meek and lowly in heart:
and ye shall find rest unto your souls."
(Matthew 11:29)

Notes

"But he said, Yea rather, blessed are they
that hear the word of God, and keep it."
(Luke 11:28)

Date:_____Speaker:_____

Topic: _____

_____

_____

_____

_____

_____

_____

_____

_____

_____

_____

_____

_____

_____

_____

_____

"Take my yoke upon you, and learn of me;
for I am meek and lowly in heart:
and ye shall find rest unto your souls."
(Matthew 11:29)

"But what saith it? The word is nigh thee, even in thy mouth, and in thy heart: that is, the word of faith, which we preach."
(Romans 10:8)

Date:_____Speaker:_____

Topic: _____

_____

_____

_____

_____

_____

_____

_____

_____

_____

_____

_____

_____

_____

_____

_____

"Take my yoke upon you, and learn of me;
for I am meek and lowly in heart:
and ye shall find rest unto your souls."
(Matthew 11:29)

Notes

"Heaven and earth shall pass away:
but my words shall not pass away."
(Mark 13:31)

Date:_____Speaker:_____

Topic: _____

_____

_____

_____

_____

_____

_____

_____

_____

_____

_____

_____

_____

_____

_____

"Take my yoke upon you, and learn of me;
for I am meek and lowly in heart:
and ye shall find rest unto your souls."
(Matthew 11:29)

Notes

"My son, if thou wilt receive my words, and hide my commandments
with thee; So that thou incline thine ear unto wisdom,
and apply thine heart to understanding."
(Proverbs 2:1-2)

Date:_____Speaker:_____

Topic: _____

_____

_____

_____

_____

_____

_____

_____

_____

_____

_____

_____

_____

_____

_____

_____

*"Take my yoke upon you, and learn of me;
for I am meek and lowly in heart:
and ye shall find rest unto your souls."*
(Matthew 11:29)

"Then opened he their understanding,
that they might understand the scriptures."
(Luke 24:45)

Date:_____ Speaker:_____

Topic: _____

_____

_____

_____

_____

_____

_____

_____

_____

_____

_____

_____

_____

_____

_____

_____

_____

"Take my yoke upon you, and learn of me;
for I am meek and lowly in heart:
and ye shall find rest unto your souls."
(Matthew 11:29)

"Let not mercy and truth forsake thee: bind them about thy neck;
write them upon the table of thine heart:"
(Proverbs 3:3)

Date:_____Speaker:_____

Topic: _____

_____

_____

_____

_____

_____

_____

_____

_____

_____

_____

_____

_____

_____

_____

_____

_____

"Take my yoke upon you, and learn of me;
for I am meek and lowly in heart:
and ye shall find rest unto your souls."
(Matthew 11:29)

Notes

"Every word of God is pure:
he is a shield unto them that put their trust in him."
(Proverbs 30:5)

Date:_____Speaker:_____

Topic: _____

_____

_____

_____

_____

_____

_____

_____

_____

_____

_____

_____

_____

_____

_____

_____

_____

"Take my yoke upon you, and learn of me;
for I am meek and lowly in heart:
and ye shall find rest unto your souls."
(Matthew 11:29)

Notes

"Let the word of Christ dwell in you richly in all wisdom; teaching and admonishing one another in psalms and hymns and spiritual songs, singing with grace in your hearts to the Lord."
(Colossians 3:16)

Date:_____Speaker:_____

Topic: _____

_____

_____

_____

_____

_____

_____

_____

_____

_____

_____

_____

_____

_____

_____

_____

_____

_____

"Take my yoke upon you, and learn of me;
for I am meek and lowly in heart:
and ye shall find rest unto your souls."
(Matthew 11:29)

Notes

"In the beginning was the Word, and the Word
was with God, and the Word was God."
(John 1:1)

Date:_____Speaker:_____

Topic: _____

_____

_____

_____

_____

_____

_____

_____

_____

_____

_____

_____

_____

_____

_____

_____

"Take my yoke upon you, and learn of me;
for I am meek and lowly in heart:
and ye shall find rest unto your souls."
(Matthew 11:29)

Notes

"Thy word is a lamp unto my feet,
and a light unto my path."
(Psalm 119:105)

Date:_____Speaker:_____

Topic: _____

_____

_____

_____

_____

_____

_____

_____

_____

_____

_____

_____

_____

_____

_____

_____

_____

*"Take my yoke upon you, and learn of me;
for I am meek and lowly in heart:
and ye shall find rest unto your souls."
(Matthew 11:29)*

Notes

"Thou art my hiding place and my shield:
I hope in thy word."
(Psalm 119:114)

Date:_____Speaker:_____

Topic: _____

_____

_____

_____

_____

_____

_____

_____

_____

_____

_____

_____

_____

_____

_____

_____

"Take my yoke upon you, and learn of me;
for I am meek and lowly in heart:
and ye shall find rest unto your souls."
(Matthew 11:29)

"My son, attend to my words;
incline thine ear unto my sayings."
(Proverbs 4:20)

Date:_____Speaker:_____

Topic: _____

_____

_____

_____

_____

_____

_____

_____

_____

_____

_____

_____

_____

_____

_____

_____

_____

*"Take my yoke upon you, and learn of me;
for I am meek and lowly in heart:
and ye shall find rest unto your souls."
(Matthew 11:29)*

But his delight is in the law of the Lord;
and in his law doth he mediate day and night."
(Psalm 1:2)

Date:_____Speaker:_____

Topic: _____

_____

_____

_____

_____

_____

_____

_____

_____

_____

_____

_____

_____

_____

_____

_____

_____

"Take my yoke upon you, and learn of me;
for I am meek and lowly in heart:
and ye shall find rest unto your souls."
(Matthew 11:29)

Notes

"Blessed is the man that walketh not in the counsel of the ungodly, nor standeth in the way of sinners, nor sitteth in the seat of the scornful."
(Psalm 1:1)

Date:_____Speaker:_____

Topic: _____

_____

_____

_____

_____

_____

_____

_____

_____

_____

_____

_____

_____

_____

_____

_____

"Take my yoke upon you, and learn of me;
for I am meek and lowly in heart:
and ye shall find rest unto your souls."
(Matthew 11:29)

"And they were astonished at his doctrine:
for his word was with power."
(Luke 4:32)

Date:_____Speaker:_____

Topic: _____

_____

_____

_____

_____

_____

_____

_____

_____

_____

_____

_____

_____

_____

_____

_____

*"Take my yoke upon you, and learn of me;
for I am meek and lowly in heart:
and ye shall find rest unto your souls."
(Matthew 11:29)*

Notes

"The entrance of thy words giveth light; it giveth
understanding unto the simple."
(Psalm 119:130)

Date:_____Speaker:_____

Topic: _____

_____

_____

_____

_____

_____

_____

_____

_____

_____

_____

_____

_____

_____

_____

_____

_____

"Take my yoke upon you, and learn of me;
for I am meek and lowly in heart:
and ye shall find rest unto your souls."
(Matthew 11:29)

Notes

"And these are they which are sown on good ground;
such as hear the word, and receive it, and bring forth fruit,
some thirtyfold, some sixty, and some an hundred."
(Mark 4:20)

Date:_____Speaker:_____

Topic: _____

_____

_____

_____

_____

_____

_____

_____

_____

_____

_____

_____

_____

_____

_____

_____

_____

"Take my yoke upon you, and learn of me;
for I am meek and lowly in heart:
and ye shall find rest unto your souls."
(Matthew 11:29)

"For the commandment is a lamp; and the law is light;
and reproofs of instruction are the way of life."
(Proverbs 6:23)

Date:_____Speaker:_____

Topic: _____

_____

_____

_____

_____

_____

_____

_____

_____

_____

_____

_____

_____

_____

_____

_____

"Take my yoke upon you, and learn of me;
for I am meek and lowly in heart:
and ye shall find rest unto your souls."
(Matthew 11:29)

Notes

"Thy word have I hid in mine heart,
that I might not sin against thee."
(Psalm 119:11)

Date:_____Speaker:_____

Topic: _____

_____

_____

_____

_____

_____

_____

_____

_____

_____

_____

_____

_____

_____

_____

_____

"Take my yoke upon you, and learn of me;
for I am meek and lowly in heart:
and ye shall find rest unto your souls."
(Matthew 11:29)

Notes

"Is not my word like as a fire? saith the LORD;
and like a hammer that breaketh the rock in pieces?"
(Jeremiah 23:29)

Date:_____Speaker:_____

Topic: _____

_____

_____

_____

_____

_____

_____

_____

_____

_____

_____

_____

_____

_____

_____

_____

"Take my yoke upon you, and learn of me;
for I am meek and lowly in heart:
and ye shall find rest unto your souls."
(Matthew 11:29)

"Teach me, O LORD, the way of thy statutes;
and I shall keep it unto the end."
(Psalm 119:33)

Date:_____Speaker:_____

Topic: _____

_____

_____

_____

_____

_____

_____

_____

_____

_____

_____

_____

_____

_____

_____

_____

"Take my yoke upon you, and learn of me;
for I am meek and lowly in heart:
and ye shall find rest unto your souls."
(Matthew 11:29)

"For the word of God is quick, and powerful, and sharper than any twoedged sword, piercing even to the dividing asunder of soul and spirit, and of the joints and marrow, and is a discerner of the thoughts and intents of the heart."
(Hebrews 4:12)

Date:_____Speaker:_____

Topic: _____

_____

_____

_____

_____

_____

_____

_____

_____

_____

_____

_____

_____

_____

_____

_____

_____

"Take my yoke upon you, and learn of me;
for I am meek and lowly in heart:
and ye shall find rest unto your souls."
(Matthew 11:29)

Notes

"For whatsoever things were written aforetime
were written for our learning, that we through patience
and comfort of the scriptures might have hope."
(Romans 15:4)

Date:_____Speaker:_____

Topic: _____

_____

_____

_____

_____

_____

_____

_____

_____

_____

_____

_____

_____

_____

_____

*"Take my yoke upon you, and learn of me;
for I am meek and lowly in heart:
and ye shall find rest unto your souls."
(Matthew 11:29)*

"Finally, my brethren, be strong in the Lord,
and in the power of his might."
(Ephesians 6:10)

Date:_____Speaker:_____

Topic: _____

_____

_____

_____

_____

_____

_____

_____

_____

_____

_____

_____

_____

_____

_____

_____

"Take my yoke upon you, and learn of me;
for I am meek and lowly in heart:
and ye shall find rest unto your souls."
(Matthew 11:29)

Notes

"He that believeth on me, as the scripture hath said,
out of his belly shall flow rivers of living water."
(John 7:38)

Date:_____Speaker:_____

Topic: _____

_____

_____

_____

_____

_____

_____

_____

_____

_____

_____

_____

_____

_____

_____

_____

_____

"Take my yoke upon you, and learn of me;
for I am meek and lowly in heart:
and ye shall find rest unto your souls."
(Matthew 11:29)

"The words of the LORD are pure words: as silver
tried in a furnace of earth, purified seven times."
(Psalm 12:6)

Date:_____Speaker:_____

Topic: _____

_____

_____

_____

_____

_____

_____

_____

_____

_____

_____

_____

_____

_____

_____

_____

_____

"Take my yoke upon you, and learn of me;
for I am meek and lowly in heart:
and ye shall find rest unto your souls."
(Matthew 11:29)

Notes

"Jesus answered and said unto him, If a man love me, he will keep my words: and my Father will love him, and we will come unto him, and make our abode with him."
(John 14:23)

Date:_____Speaker:_____

Topic: _____

_____

_____

_____

_____

_____

_____

_____

_____

_____

_____

_____

_____

_____

_____

_____

"Take my yoke upon you, and learn of me;
for I am meek and lowly in heart:
and ye shall find rest unto your souls."
(Matthew 11:29)

Notes

"Show me thy ways, O LORD; teach me thy paths."
(Psalm 25:4)

Date:_____Speaker:_____

Topic: _____

_____

_____

_____

_____

_____

_____

_____

_____

_____

_____

_____

_____

_____

_____

_____

_____

_____

"Take my yoke upon you, and learn of me;
for I am meek and lowly in heart:
and ye shall find rest unto your souls."
(Matthew 11:29)

Notes

"Teaching them to observe all things whatsoever I have commanded you: and, lo, I am with you always, even unto the end of the world. Amen."
(Matthew 28:20)

Date:_____Speaker:_____

Topic: _____

_____

_____

_____

_____

_____

_____

_____

_____

_____

_____

_____

_____

_____

_____

"Take my yoke upon you, and learn of me;
for I am meek and lowly in heart:
and ye shall find rest unto your souls."
(Matthew 11:29)

Notes

"And the Word was made flesh, and dwelt among us, (and we beheld his glory, the glory as of the only begotten of the Father,) full of grace and truth." (John 1:14)

Date:_____Speaker:_____

Topic: _____

_____

_____

_____

_____

_____

_____

_____

_____

_____

_____

_____

_____

_____

_____

_____

_____

"Take my yoke upon you, and learn of me;
for I am meek and lowly in heart:
and ye shall find rest unto your souls."
(Matthew 11:29)

Notes

"The simple believeth every word:
but the prudent man looketh well to his going."
(Proverbs 14:15)

Date:_____Speaker:_____

Topic: _____

_____

_____

_____

_____

_____

_____

_____

_____

_____

_____

_____

_____

_____

_____

_____

_____

"Take my yoke upon you, and learn of me;
for I am meek and lowly in heart:
and ye shall find rest unto your souls."
(Matthew 11:29)

"Therefore whosoever heareth these sayings of mine, and doeth them,
I will liken him unto a wise man, which built his house upon a rock:"
(Matthew 7:24)

Date:_____Speaker:_____

Topic: _____

_____

_____

_____

_____

_____

_____

_____

_____

_____

_____

_____

_____

_____

_____

_____

_____

"Take my yoke upon you, and learn of me;
for I am meek and lowly in heart:
and ye shall find rest unto your souls."
(Matthew 11:29)

Notes

"For the word of the LORD is right;
and all his works are done in truth."
(Psalm 33:4)

Date:_____Speaker:_____

Topic: _____

_____

_____

_____

_____

_____

_____

_____

_____

_____

_____

_____

_____

_____

_____

_____

_____

"Take my yoke upon you, and learn of me;
for I am meek and lowly in heart:
and ye shall find rest unto your souls."
(Matthew 11:29)

"The name of the LORD is a strong tower:
the righteous runneth into it, and is safe."
(Proverbs 18:10)

Date:_____Speaker:_____

Topic: _____

_____

_____

_____

_____

_____

_____

_____

_____

_____

_____

_____

_____

_____

_____

_____

*"Take my yoke upon you, and learn of me;
for I am meek and lowly in heart:
and ye shall find rest unto your souls."
(Matthew 11:29)*

Notes

"I am come a light into the world, that whosoever
believeth on me should not abide in darkness."
(John 12:46)

Date:_____Speaker:_____

Topic: _____

_____

_____

_____

_____

_____

_____

_____

_____

_____

_____

_____

_____

_____

_____

_____

_____

"Take my yoke upon you, and learn of me;
for I am meek and lowly in heart:
and ye shall find rest unto your souls."
(Matthew 11:29)

Notes

"I will delight myself in thy statues:
I will not forget thy word."
(Psalm 119:16)

Date:_____Speaker:_____

Topic: _____

_____

_____

_____

_____

_____

_____

_____

_____

_____

_____

_____

_____

_____

_____

_____

"Take my yoke upon you, and learn of me;
for I am meek and lowly in heart:
and ye shall find rest unto your souls."
(Matthew 11:29)

Notes

"Now ye are clean through the word which
I have spoken unto you."
(John 15:3)

Date:_____ Speaker:_____

Topic: _____

_____

_____

_____

_____

_____

_____

_____

_____

_____

_____

_____

_____

_____

_____

_____

"Take my yoke upon you, and learn of me;
for I am meek and lowly in heart:
and ye shall find rest unto your souls."
(Matthew 11:29)

Notes

"Make me to understand the way of thy precepts:
so shall I talk of thy wondrous works. My soul melteth for heaviness:
strengthen thou me according unto thy word."
(Psalm 119:27-28)

Date:_____Speaker:_____

Topic: _____

_____

_____

_____

_____

_____

_____

_____

_____

_____

_____

_____

_____

_____

_____

_____

_____

"Take my yoke upon you, and learn of me;
for I am meek and lowly in heart:
and ye shall find rest unto your souls."
(Matthew 11:29)

Notes

"Sanctify them through thy truth: thy word is truth; As thou hast sent me into the world, even so have I also sent them into the world."
(John 17:17-18)

Date:_____Speaker:_____

Topic: _____

_____

_____

_____

_____

_____

_____

_____

_____

_____

_____

_____

_____

_____

_____

_____

"Take my yoke upon you, and learn of me;
for I am meek and lowly in heart:
and ye shall find rest unto your souls."
(Matthew 11:29)

Notes

"Seek ye the Lord while he may be found,
call ye upon him while he is near:"
(Isaiah 55:6)

Date:_____Speaker:_____

Topic: _____

_____

_____

_____

_____

_____

_____

_____

_____

_____

_____

_____

_____

_____

_____

"Take my yoke upon you, and learn of me;
for I am meek and lowly in heart:
and ye shall find rest unto your souls."
(Matthew 11:29)

"That he might sanctify and cleanse it with
the washing of water by the word."
(Ephesians 5:26)

Date:_____Speaker:_____

Topic: _____

_____

_____

_____

_____

_____

_____

_____

_____

_____

_____

_____

_____

_____

_____

_____

"Take my yoke upon you, and learn of me;
for I am meek and lowly in heart:
and ye shall find rest unto your souls."
(Matthew 11:29)

Notes

"So shall my word be that goeth forth out of my mouth: it shall not return unto me void, but it shall accomplish that which I please, and it shall prosper in the thing whereto I sent it."
(Isaiah 55:11)

Date:_____Speaker:_____

Topic: _____

_____

_____

_____

_____

_____

_____

_____

_____

_____

_____

_____

_____

_____

_____

_____

_____

"Take my yoke upon you, and learn of me;
for I am meek and lowly in heart:
and ye shall find rest unto your souls."
(Matthew 11:29)

"Search the scriptures; for in them ye think ye have eternal life:
and they are they which testify of me."
(John 5:39)

Date:_____Speaker:_____

Topic: _____

_____

_____

_____

_____

_____

_____

_____

_____

_____

_____

_____

_____

_____

_____

_____

_____

"Take my yoke upon you, and learn of me;
for I am meek and lowly in heart:
and ye shall find rest unto your souls."
(Matthew 11:29)

Notes

"Verily, verily, I say unto you, He that heareth my word,
and believeth on him that sent me, hath everlasting life, and shall
not come into condemnation: but is passed from death unto life."
(John 5:24)

Date:_____Speaker:_____

Topic: _____

_____

_____

_____

_____

_____

_____

_____

_____

_____

_____

_____

_____

_____

_____

_____

_____

"Take my yoke upon you, and learn of me;
for I am meek and lowly in heart:
and ye shall find rest unto your souls."
(Matthew 11:29)

Notes

"Heaven and earth shall pass away:
but my words shall not pass away."
(Luke 21:33)

Date:_____Speaker:_____

Topic: _____

_____

_____

_____

_____

_____

_____

_____

_____

_____

_____

_____

_____

_____

_____

_____

"Take my yoke upon you, and learn of me;
for I am meek and lowly in heart:
and ye shall find rest unto your souls."
(Matthew 11:29)

"Wherewithal shall a young man cleanse his way?
By taking heed thereto according to thy word."
(Psalm 119:9)

Date:_____Speaker:_____

Topic: _____

_____

_____

_____

_____

_____

_____

_____

_____

_____

_____

_____

_____

_____

_____

_____

_____

"Take my yoke upon you, and learn of me;
for I am meek and lowly in heart:
and ye shall find rest unto your souls."
(Matthew 11:29)

Notes

"Jesus answered and said unto them, Ye do err,
not knowing the scriptures, nor the power of God."
(Matthew 22:29)

Date:_____Speaker:_____

Topic: _____

_____

_____

_____

_____

_____

_____

_____

_____

_____

_____

_____

_____

_____

_____

_____

_____

"Take my yoke upon you, and learn of me;
for I am meek and lowly in heart:
and ye shall find rest unto your souls."
(Matthew 11:29)

Notes

"As for God, his way is perfect; the word of the LORD is tried:
he is a buckler to all them that trust in him."
(2 Samuel 22:31)

Date:_____Speaker:_____

Topic: _____

_____

_____

_____

_____

_____

_____

_____

_____

_____

_____

_____

_____

_____

_____

_____

_____

_____

"Take my yoke upon you, and learn of me;
for I am meek and lowly in heart:
and ye shall find rest unto your souls."
(Matthew 11:29)

"But if the gospel be hid, it is hid to them that are lost."
(2 Corinthians 4:3)

Date:_____Speaker:_____

Topic: _____

_____

_____

_____

_____

_____

_____

_____

_____

_____

_____

_____

_____

_____

_____

_____

"Take my yoke upon you, and learn of me;
for I am meek and lowly in heart:
and ye shall find rest unto your souls."
(Matthew 11:29)

"So then faith cometh by hearing, and hearing by the word of God."
(Romans 10:17)

Date:_____Speaker:_____

Topic: _____

_____

_____

_____

_____

_____

_____

_____

_____

_____

_____

_____

_____

_____

_____

_____

"Take my yoke upon you, and learn of me;
for I am meek and lowly in heart:
and ye shall find rest unto your souls."
(Matthew 11:29)

Notes

"It is the spirit that quickeneth; the flesh profiteth nothing: the words
that I speak unto you, they are spirit, and they are life."
(John 6:63)

Date:_____Speaker:_____

Topic: _____

_____

_____

_____

_____

_____

_____

_____

_____

_____

_____

_____

_____

_____

_____

_____

_____

_____

"Take my yoke upon you, and learn of me;
for I am meek and lowly in heart:
and ye shall find rest unto your souls."
(Matthew 11:29)

Notes

"But he answered and said, It is written, Man shall not live by bread alone, but by every word that proceedeth out of the mouth of God."
(Matthew 4:4)

Date:_____ Speaker:_____

Topic: _____

_____

_____

_____

_____

_____

_____

_____

_____

_____

_____

_____

_____

_____

_____

_____

_____

"Take my yoke upon you, and learn of me;
for I am meek and lowly in heart:
and ye shall find rest unto your souls."
(Matthew 11:29)

Notes

"Holding fast the faithful word as he hath been taught, that he may be able by sound doctrine both to exhort and to convince the gainsayers."
(Titus 1:9)

Date:_____Speaker:_____

Topic: _____

_____

_____

_____

_____

_____

_____

_____

_____

_____

_____

_____

_____

_____

_____

_____

"Take my yoke upon you, and learn of me;
for I am meek and lowly in heart:
and ye shall find rest unto your souls."
(Matthew 11:29)

"Let us therefore come boldly unto the throne of grace, that we may
obtain mercy, and find grace to help in time of need."
(Hebrews 4:16)

Date:_____Speaker:_____

Topic: _____

_____

_____

_____

_____

_____

_____

_____

_____

_____

_____

_____

_____

_____

_____

_____

_____

"Take my yoke upon you, and learn of me;
for I am meek and lowly in heart:
and ye shall find rest unto your souls."
(Matthew 11:29)

Notes

"But be ye doers of the word, and not hearers only,
deceiving your own selves."
(James 1:22)

Date:_____Speaker:_____

Topic: _____

_____

_____

_____

_____

_____

_____

_____

_____

_____

_____

_____

_____

_____

_____

_____

_____

"Take my yoke upon you, and learn of me;
for I am meek and lowly in heart:
and ye shall find rest unto your souls."
(Matthew 11:29)

"By the word of the LORD were the heavens made;
and all the host of them by the breath of his mouth."
(Psalm 33:6)

Date:_____Speaker:_____

Topic: _____

_____

_____

_____

_____

_____

_____

_____

_____

_____

_____

_____

_____

_____

_____

_____

"Take my yoke upon you, and learn of me;
for I am meek and lowly in heart:
and ye shall find rest unto your souls."
(Matthew 11:29)

Notes

"As newborn babes, desire the sincere milk of the word,
that ye may grow thereby."
(1 Peter 2:2)

Date:_____Speaker:_____

Topic: _____

_____

_____

_____

_____

_____

_____

_____

_____

_____

_____

_____

_____

_____

_____

_____

_____

"Take my yoke upon you, and learn of me;
for I am meek and lowly in heart:
and ye shall find rest unto your souls."
(Matthew 11:29)

Notes

"For I am not ashamed of the gospel of Christ: for it is the power of God unto salvation to every one that believeth: to the Jew first, and also to the Greek."
(Romans 1:16)

Date:_____Speaker:_____

Topic: _____

_____

_____

_____

_____

_____

_____

_____

_____

_____

_____

_____

_____

_____

_____

_____

_____

"Take my yoke upon you, and learn of me;
for I am meek and lowly in heart:
and ye shall find rest unto your souls."
(Matthew 11:29)

Notes

"But whoso keepeth his word, in him verily is the love of God perfected: hereby know we that we are in him."
(1 John 2:5)

Date:_____ Speaker:_____

Topic: _____

_____

_____

_____

_____

_____

_____

_____

_____

_____

_____

_____

_____

_____

_____

_____

_____

"Take my yoke upon you, and learn of me;
for I am meek and lowly in heart:
and ye shall find rest unto your souls."
(Matthew 11:29)

"He that saith he abideth in him ought himself also so to walk,
even as he walked."
(1 John 2:6)

Date:_____Speaker:_____

Topic: _____

_____

_____

_____

_____

_____

_____

_____

_____

_____

_____

_____

_____

_____

_____

_____

_____

"Take my yoke upon you, and learn of me;
for I am meek and lowly in heart:
and ye shall find rest unto your souls."
(Matthew 11:29)

Notes

"Blessed is he that readeth, and they that hear the words of this prophecy, and keep those things which are written therein: for the time is at hand." (Revelation 1:3)

Date:_____Speaker:_____

Topic: _____

_____

_____

_____

_____

_____

_____

_____

_____

_____

_____

_____

_____

_____

_____

_____

"Take my yoke upon you, and learn of me;
for I am meek and lowly in heart:
and ye shall find rest unto your souls."
(Matthew 11:29)

Notes

"My sheep hear my voice, and I know them and they follow me:"
(John 10:27)

Date:_____Speaker:_____

Topic: _____

_____

_____

_____

_____

_____

_____

_____

_____

_____

_____

_____

_____

_____

_____

_____

_____

"Take my yoke upon you, and learn of me;
for I am meek and lowly in heart:
and ye shall find rest unto your souls."
(Matthew 11:29)

Notes

"Let us hear the conclusion of the whole matter: Fear God, and keep his commandments: for this is the whole duty of man."
(Ecclesiastes 12:13)

Date:_____Speaker:_____

Topic: _____

_____

_____

_____

_____

_____

_____

_____

_____

_____

_____

_____

_____

_____

_____

_____

_____

"Take my yoke upon you, and learn of me;
for I am meek and lowly in heart:
and ye shall find rest unto your souls."
(Matthew 11:29)

Prayer

"Be careful for nothing;
but in every thing by prayer and supplication
with thanksgiving let your requests
be made known unto God."
Philippians 4:6

God Hears Me in Prayer

Record the blessings of the Lord
manifested as a result of prayer

Prayer is a Weapon

**"Give ear to my prayer, O God;
and hide not thyself from my supplication."
(Psalm 55:1)**

Prayer is so essential in our lives. Even Jesus had to pray to the Father for himself, his disciples and us. It is important that we follow the roadmap of Jesus' and Paul's prayers for the church. Jesus spoke a parable in Luke 18:1 that men ought to always pray and not faint. Paul realized the importance of praying for the Body of Believers by encouraging them to remain steadfast in prayer. We should make praying and communicating with God a top priority in our life.

Lord's Prayer (Matthew 6:9-15)

Our Father which art in heaven, Hallowed be thy name. Thy kingdom come, Thy will be done in earth, as it is in heaven. Give us this day our daily bread. And forgive us our debts, as we forgive our debtors. And lead us not into temptation, but deliver us from evil: For thine is the kingdom, and the power, and the glory, forever. Amen.

Jesus Prayed to the Father (Matthew 26:39, 42)

Going a little farther, he fell with his face to the ground and prayed, "My Father, if it is possible, may this cup be taken from me. Yet not as I will, but as you will." He went away a second time and prayed, "My Father, if it is not possible for this cup to be taken away unless I drink it, may your will be done."

Prayer is a Weapon

**"Give ear to my prayer, O God;
and hide not thyself from my supplication."
(Psalm 55:1)**

⊱⊰

Jesus Christ Intercessor Prayer (John 17:20-26)

My prayer is not for them alone. I pray also for those who will believe in me through their message, that all of them may be one, Father, just as you are in me and I am in you. May they also be in us so that the world may believe that you have sent me. I have given them the glory that you gave me, that they may be one as we are one. I in them and you in me—so that they may be brought to complete unity. Then the world will know that you sent me and have loved them even as you have loved me. Father, I want those you have given me to be with me where I am, and to see my glory, the glory you have given me because you loved me before the creation of the world. Righteous Father, though the world does not know you, I know you, and they know that you have sent me. I have made you known to them, and will continue to make you known in order that the love you have for me may be in them and that I myself may be in them.

⊱⊰

Jesus Prayed for His Disciples (John 17: 9)

I pray for them. I am not praying for the world, but for those you have given me, for they are yours. All I have is yours, and all you have is mine. And glory has come to me through them. I will remain in the world no longer, but they are still in the world, and I am coming to you. Holy Father, protect them by the power of your name, the name you gave me, so that they may be one as we are one. While I was with them, I protected them and kept them safe by that name you gave me. None has been lost except the one doomed to destruction so that Scripture would be fulfilled.

Prayer is a Weapon

"Let my prayer come before thee: incline thine ear unto my cry." Psalm 88:2

❧

Prayer of Hope (Romans 15:5-6, 13)

Now the God of patience and consolation grant you to be likeminded one toward another according to Christ Jesus: That ye may with one mind and one mouth glorify God, even the Father of our Lord Jesus Christ.

Now the God of hope fill you with all joy and peace in believing, that ye may abound in hope, through the power of the Holy Ghost.

❧

Prayer of Comfort (2 Corinthians 1:3-4)

Blessed be God, even the Father of our Lord Jesus Christ, the Father of mercies, and the God of all comfort; Who comforteth us in all our tribulation, that we may be able to comfort them which are in any trouble, by the comfort wherewith we ourselves are comforted of God.

❧

Prayer of Knowing God's Will (Colossians 1:9-12)

For this reason, since the day we heard about you, we have not stopped praying for you. We continually ask God to fill you with the knowledge of his will through all the wisdom and understanding that the Spirit gives, so that you may live a life worthy of the Lord and please him in every way: bearing fruit in every good work, growing in the knowledge of God, being strengthened with all power according to his glorious might so that you may have great endurance and patience, and giving joyful thanks to the Father, who has qualified you to share in the inheritance of his holy people in the kingdom of light.

Prayer is a Weapon

"Let my prayer come before thee:
incline thine ear unto my cry." Psalm 88:2

Prayer of Inner Strength (Ephesians 3:14-21)

For this reason I kneel before the Father, from whom every family in heaven and on earth derives its name. I pray that out of his glorious riches he may strengthen you with power through his Spirit in your inner being, so that Christ may dwell in your hearts through faith. And I pray that you, being rooted and established in love, may have power, together with all the Lord's holy people, to grasp how wide and long and high and deep is the love of Christ, and to know this love that surpasses knowledge that you may be filled to the measure of all the fullness of God. Now to him who is able to do immeasurably more than all we ask or imagine, according to his power that is at work within us, to him be glory in the church and in Christ Jesus throughout all generations, forever and ever! Amen.

Prayer of Doing God's Will (Hebrews 13:20-21)

Now the God of peace, that brought again from the dead our Lord Jesus, that great shepherd of the sheep, through the blood of the everlasting covenant, Make you perfect in every good work to do his will, working in you that which is wellpleasing in his sight, through Jesus Christ; to whom be glory for ever and ever. Amen.

Prayer is a Weapon

**"For the eyes of the LORD are over the righteous,
and his ears are open unto their prayers: but the
face of the LORD is against them that do evil."
(I Peter 3:12)**

Prayer for Spiritual Wisdom (Ephesians 1:15-23)

For this reason, ever since I heard about your faith in the Lord Jesus and your love for all God's people, I have not stopped giving thanks for you, remembering you in my prayers. I keep asking that the God of our Lord Jesus Christ, the glorious Father, may give you the Spirit of wisdom and revelation, so that you may know him better. I pray that the eyes of your heart may be enlightened in order that you may know the hope to which he has called you, the riches of his glorious inheritance in his holy people, and his incomparably great power for us who believe. That power is the same as the mighty strength he exerted when he raised Christ from the dead and seated him at his right hand in the heavenly realms, far above all rule and authority, power and dominion, and every name that is invoked, not only in the present age but also in the one to come. And God placed all things under his feet and appointed him to be head over everything for the church, which is his body, the fullness of him who fills everything in every way.

Prayer of Adoration (1 Chronicles 29:10-13)

Praise be to you, LORD, the God of our father Israel, from everlasting to everlasting. Yours, LORD, is the greatness and the power and the glory and the majesty and the splendor, for everything in heaven and earth is yours. Yours, LORD, is the kingdom; you are exalted as head over all. Wealth and honor come from you; you are the ruler of all things. In your hands are strength and power to exalt and give strength to all. Now, our God, we give you thanks, and praise your glorious name.

Prayer is a Weapon

**"And whatsoever we ask, we receive of him,
because we keep his commandments,
and do those things that are pleasing in his sight."
(1 John 3:22)**

Prayer of Wisdom (James 1:5-6)

If any of you lacks wisdom, you should ask God, who gives generously to all without finding fault, and it will be given to you. But when you ask, you must believe and not doubt, because the one who doubts is like a wave of the sea, blown and tossed by the wind.

Prayer of Love (Philippians 1:9-11)

And this is my prayer: that your love may abound more and more in knowledge and depth of insight, so that you may be able to discern what is best and may be pure and blameless for the day of Christ, filled with the fruit of righteousness that comes through Jesus Christ—to the glory and praise of God.

God loves us so much that He allowed His only Son to be a ransom for our sin. So, why not spend some time alone with God and communicate with Him. He wants to hear from you.

God Hears Me in Prayer

"For with the heart man believeth unto righteousness;
and with the mouth confession is made unto salvation."
(Romans 10:10)

Date	Prayer Petitions and Answers

*"Be careful for nothing; but in every thing by prayer and supplication with
thanksgiving let your requests be made known unto God."*

(Philippians 4:6)

God Hears Me in Prayer

"For with the heart man believeth unto righteousness;
and with the mouth confession is made unto salvation."
(Romans 10:10)

Date	Prayer Petitions and Answers

*"Be careful for nothing; but in every thing by prayer and supplication with
thanksgiving let your requests be made known unto God."*

(Philippians 4:6)

God Hears Me in Prayer

"Let my prayer come before thee:
incline thine ear unto my cry."
(Psalm 88:2)

Date	Prayer Petitions and Answers

*"Be careful for nothing; but in every thing by prayer and supplication with
thanksgiving let your requests be made known unto God."*

(Philippians 4:6)

God Hears Me in Prayer

"Give ear to my prayer, O God;
and hide not thyself from my supplication."
(Psalm 88:2)

Date	Prayer Petitions and Answers

*"Be careful for nothing; but in every thing by prayer and supplication with
thanksgiving let your requests be made known unto God."*

(Philippians 4:6)

Witness

"Let your light so shine
before men, that they may see
your good works, and glorify
your Father which is in heaven."
(Matthew 5:16)

Witness

You are the light of the world

Be encouraged and eager to share the
Word of God by continuously hearing,
believing, obeying, and trusting in the Word.

Hearing the Word of God will cause your faith to come alive. Believing the Word of God will cause you to act on it. Obeying the Word of God will cause you to prosper. Trusting the Word of God will allow the power of the Holy Spirit to perform the mission assigned to you.

Therefore, go forth and do what God has assigned you to do and evangelize. "Go ye therefore, and teach all nations, baptizing them in the name of the Father, and of the Son, and of the Holy Ghost." (Matthew 28:19)

❖ Realize who you are in Jesus Christ

"Ye are the light of the world. A city that is set on a hill cannot be hid." Neither do men light a candle, and put it under a bushel, but on a candlestick; and it giveth light unto all that are in the house. Let your light so shine before men, that they may see your good works, and glorify your Father which is in heaven." **(Matthew 5:14)**

"But ye are a chosen generation, a royal priesthood, an holy nation, a peculiar people; that ye should shew forth the praises of him who hath called you out of darkness into his marvellous light; Which in time past were not a people, but are now the people of God: which had not obtained mercy, but now have obtained mercy." **(1 Peter 2:9-10)**

"Now then we are ambassadors for Christ, as though God did beseech you by us: we pray you in Christ's stead, be ye reconciled to God. For he hath made him to be sin for us, who knew no sin; that we might be made the righteousness of God in him." **(2 Corinthians 5:20-21)**

❖ Realize your mission in winning souls

"So God created man in his own image, in the image of God created he him; male and female created he them. And God blessed them, and God said unto them, Be fruitful, and multiply, and replenish the earth, and subdue it: and have dominion over the fish of the sea, and over the fowl of the air, and over every living thing that moveth upon the earth." **(Genesis 1:27-28)**

"Ye have not chosen me, but I have chosen you, and ordained you, that ye should go and bring forth fruit, and that your fruit should remain: that whatsoever ye shall ask of the Father in my name, he may give it you ." **(John 15:16)**

"Behold I send you forth as sheep in the midst of wolves: be ye therefore wise as serpents, and harmless as doves." **(Matthew 10:16)**

"And the lord said unto the servant, Go out into the highways and hedges, and compel them to come in, that my house may be filled." **(Luke 14:23)**

"Go ye therefore, and teach all nations, baptizing them in the name of the Father, and of the Son, and of the Holy Ghost." **(Matthew 28:19)**

"And he said unto them, Go ye into all the world, and preach the gospel to every creature. He that believeth and is baptized shall be saved; but he that believeth not shall be dammed. And these signs shall follow them that believe; In my name shall they cast out devils; they shall speak with new tongues; They shall take up serpents; and if they drink any deadly thing, it shall not hurt them; they shall lay hands on the sick, and they shall recover." **(Mark 16:15-18)**

Evangelistic Testimony

"When thou saidst, Seek ye my face: my heart said unto thee, Thy face, LORD, will I seek."
(Psalm 27:8)

"Let your light so shine before men, that they may see your good works, and glorify your Father which is in heaven."
(Matthew 5:16)

Evangelistic Testimony

"God, thou art my God; early will I seek thee: my soul thirsteth for thee, my flesh longeth for thee in a dry and thirsty land, where no water is."
(Psalm 63:1)

_____

_____

_____

_____

_____

_____

_____

_____

_____

_____

_____

_____

_____

_____

_____

_____

_____

_____

_____

_____

*"Let your light so shine before men, that they may see your good works,
and glorify your Father which is in heaven."
(Matthew 5:16)*

Evangelistic Testimony

With my soul have I desired thee in the night; yea, with my spirit within me will I seek thee early: for wen thy judgments are in the earth, the inhabitants of the world will learn righteousness."
(Isaiah 26:9)

_____

_____

_____

_____

_____

_____

_____

_____

_____

_____

_____

_____

_____

_____

_____

_____

_____

_____

"Let your light so shine before men, that they may see your good works, and glorify your Father which is in heaven."
(Matthew 5:16)

Evangelistic Testimony

"'Seek the LORD and his strength, seek his face continually."
(I Chronicles 16:11)

_____

_____

_____

_____

_____

_____

_____

_____

_____

_____

_____

_____

_____

_____

_____

_____

_____

_____

"Let your light so shine before men, that they may see your good works,
and glorify your Father which is in heaven."
(Matthew 5:16)

Evangelistic Testimony

"But without faith it is impossible to please him: for he that cometh
to God must believe that he is, and that he is a rewarder
of them that diligently seek him."
(Hebrews 11:6)

_____

_____

_____

_____

_____

_____

_____

_____

_____

_____

_____

_____

_____

_____

_____

_____

_____

_____

*"Let your light so shine before men, that they may see your good works,
and glorify your Father which is in heaven."
(Matthew 5:16)*

Evangelistic Testimony

"Seek ye the LORD while he may be found,
call ye upon him while he is near:"
(Isaiah 55:6)

_____

_____

_____

_____

_____

_____

_____

_____

_____

_____

_____

_____

_____

_____

_____

_____

_____

_____

_____

_____

*"Let your light so shine before men, that they may see your good works,
and glorify your Father which is in heaven."*
(Matthew 5:16)

Evangelistic Testimony

"The LORD is good unto them that wait for him,
to the soul that seeketh him."
(Lamentations 3:25)

_____

_____

_____

_____

_____

_____

_____

_____

_____

_____

_____

_____

_____

_____

_____

_____

_____

*"Let your light so shine before men, that they may see your good works,
and glorify your Father which is in heaven."*
(Matthew 5:16)

Evangelistic Testimony

"And ye shall seek me, and find me,
When ye shall search for me with all your heart."
(Jeremiah 29:13)

_____

_____

_____

_____

_____

_____

_____

_____

_____

_____

_____

_____

_____

_____

_____

_____

_____

_____

"Let your light so shine before men, that they may see your good works,
and glorify your Father which is in heaven."
(Matthew 5:16)

Evangelistic Testimony

"The young lions do lack, and suffer hunger:
but they that seek the LORD shall not want any good thing."
(Psalm 34:10)

_____

_____

_____

_____

_____

_____

_____

_____

_____

_____

_____

_____

_____

_____

_____

_____

_____

_____

*"Let your light so shine before men, that they may see your good works,
and glorify your Father which is in heaven."*
(Matthew 5:16)

Notes

Notes

Notes

Notes

Notes

Notes